THE ULTIMATE ANIMAL CRIMINALS

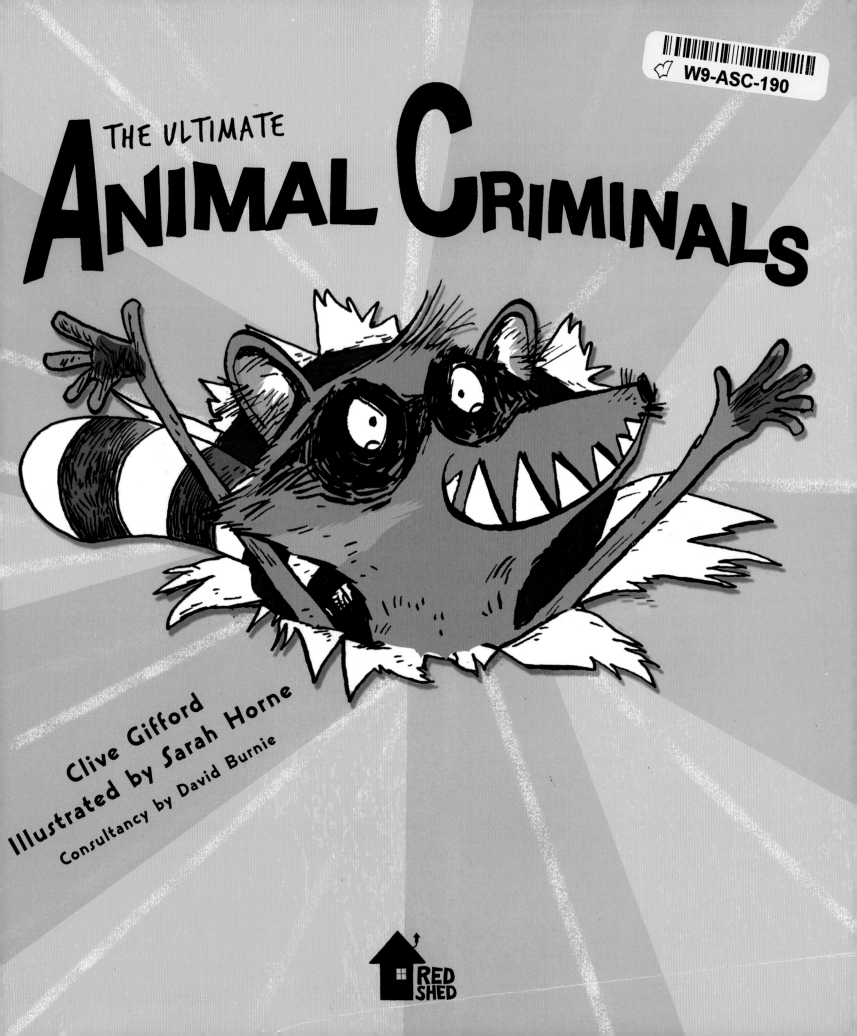

Clive Gifford
Illustrated by Sarah Horne
Consultancy by David Burnie

RED SHED

Contents

Introduction

Not all creatures play by the rules . . .

The natural world may be beautiful but it also suffers from a shockingly high crime rate: it turns out that it is packed with rotters and plotters, maulers and brawlers, and even hooligans and house wreckers!

Many creatures have found that the best way to survive is to turn to thievery or become a con artist to gain food caught by others. Others group together in wild, lawless gangs to bully and heap terror and misery on other creatures, or take over the neighbourhood. Some go it alone as stealthy assassins or bust out of captivity and go on the run, eluding people's attempts to catch them.

This book has rounded up a criminal collection of creatures who brutalise, vandalise, cheat, fake and steal. Packed within these pages are tyrant toads, looting lemurs, mischievous monkeys and many more curious creatures.

Are you ready to meet them?

Cute or Brute?

Ahhh, aren't these creatures adorable? Many living things are blessed with looks we find cute, or colours we think of as pretty. Some, though, harbour a deep, dark secret beneath their skin or fur . . . they can be deadly, vicious or violent!

All Eyes and Fur

One of the world's cutest critters is the slow loris. It lives in rainforests in southeast Asia, where it snacks on insects, fruit and leaves amongst other things. It has a super strong grip and can hang from a branch by its feet whilst feeding. The slow loris also has a vicious bite – so beware!

WATCH OUT FOR ITS TEETH! THE SLOW LORIS HAS A TOXIC BITE THAT IT USES TO PROTECT ITSELF AGAINST PREDATORS.

VENOM IS STORED IN PATCHES BY ITS ELBOWS, WHICH THE LORIS LICKS AND MIXES WITH SALIVA IN ITS MOUTH. ONE BITE CAN CAUSE A SEVERE ALLERGIC REACTION OR EVEN DEATH.

Hop It!

Poison dart frogs are found in Central and South American rainforests. There are over 170 species of these frogs and they come in a dazzling array of colours. Most are tiny – between two and four centimetres long – but they have dreadfully deadly skin.

LOOK BUT DON'T TOUCH! POISON DART FROGS ARE PRETTY BUT THEY HAVE POWERFUL POISONS ON THEIR SKIN THAT CAN HARM OR KILL.

THE POISON STRENGTH OF EACH SPECIES OF FROG VARIES: SOME FROGS CAN CAUSE SICKNESS OR MUSCLE CRAMPS, WHILST OTHERS HAVE ENOUGH VENOM TO KILL 10 ADULT HUMANS!

Snouting About

Chances are you'll find giant anteaters pretty comical looking, lovable even. Their long snouts and claws are used to dig into ant and termite nests, but their claws are used as violent weapons, too.

WHEN THREATENED, THE ANTEATER CAN DEFEND ITSELF WITH ITS BRUTAL 10-CENTIMETRE-LONG CLAWS. THESE CLAWS CAN KILL A MOUNTAIN LION OR JAGUAR – AN ANTEATER'S MAIN PREDATORS.

Masters of Disguise

Roll up! Roll up! Come and see those who copy the actions or looks of others for their own devious ends. Wanted posters just won't work with these cunning critters.

Snake Eyes

Caterpillars are popular snacks for many creatures, including birds and small rodents. However, some caterpillars, such as the elephant hawkmoth, disguise themselves as scary snakes to put off potential predators.

THE ELEPHANT HAWKMOTH CATERPILLAR PULLS IN ITS HEAD AND LEGS TO HELP SWELL ITS BODY AND APPEAR MORE LIKE A SNAKE.

CRAFTY CATERPILLAR

COMING SOON:
MIMIC MAESTROS

CAN YOU SPOT THE TWO PYGMY SEAHORSES IN THIS PHOTO?

PYGMY SEAHORSES ARE JUST TWO CENTIMETRES LONG BUT THEY HAVE A BIG DISGUISE. THEY LOOK JUST LIKE THE GORGONIAN SEA FAN, A CREATURE RELATED TO THE CORAL THAT THEY LIVE AMONGST.

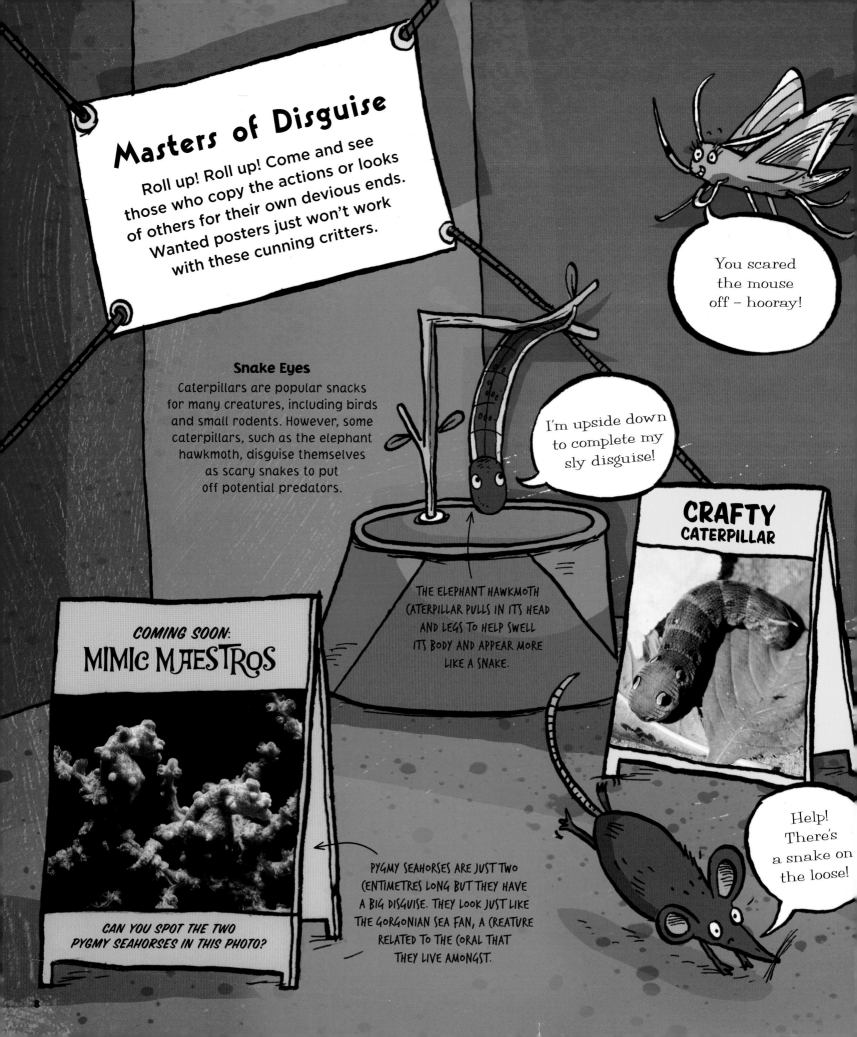

Making an Impression

With their eight arms and bulbous body, you'd think that an octopus would be the last creature to look like anything else . . . but you would be wrong. The mimic octopus *Thaumoctopus mimicus* performs incredible impressions and has quite a repertoire. Here are just some of them:

And now for my next impression . . .

Flatfish

THE OCTOPUS FLATTENS ITSELF AND DRAWS ITS ARMS TOGETHER TO LOOK LIKE A SOLE, A TYPE OF FLATFISH.

Stingray

THE BLACK-MARBLE JAWFISH COPIES THE MIMIC OCTOPUS. IT PRETENDS TO BE ONE OF THE OCTOPUS' ARMS SO THAT IT CAN SWIM CLOSE BY AND HOOVER UP ANY REMNANTS OF THE OCTOPUS' MEALS. SNEAKY!

Sea snake

THE OCTOPUS BUNDLES MOST OF ITS ARMS TOGETHER AND LETS ONE ARM TRAIL BEHIND TO LOOK LIKE A STINGRAY.

TO APPEAR AS A SEA SNAKE, THE MIMIC OCTOPUS CHANGES COLOUR TO CREATE THE SNAKE'S YELLOW AND BLACK BANDS.

Bullies

Not all bullies are human. Many are found in the natural world, too. Sometimes, members in a group of creatures battle each other to determine who should be the leader. But the really nasty brutes often pick on the weakest and sometimes this is purely for kicks.

GROUPER

Push off, small fry.

Eeeeeek!

Coral Clear Off

Young damselfish living around coral in the Great Barrier Reef have little time to admire the view, as they are often bullied by older, bigger damselfish. The bullies force them out of sheltered spots in the coral and into more open areas, where they are more likely to be eaten by fishy predators, such as groupers.

Gulp!

School Bully

Bottlenose dolphins seem friendly but some are brutal bullies. Schools of dolphins sometimes torment a lone harbour porpoise, circling round and then ramming it at high speed. Repeated ramming can cause death.

SCIENTISTS AREN'T SURE WHY DOLPHINS BULLY PORPOISES. IT CAN'T BE ABOUT FOOD BECAUSE DOLPHINS DON'T EAT PORPOISES OR COMPETE FOR MANY OF THE SAME FOODS.

Buzz Off

Fruit flies are normally calm characters, but when male fruit flies smell a chemical called 11-*cis*-vaccenyl acetate (or *c*VA for short) that's given off by other male fruit flies, they can turn nasty. They'll start bullying and attacking other males, snapping at them and driving them away.

Take That!

Some courageous creatures bravely face up to bullies and expose them for the cowards they often are. The California ground squirrel's mortal enemy is the rattlesnake. When attacked, the squirrel will kick dirt or sand at the bully, or wave its tail around to give the impression it is a much larger creature.

Sealing Their Fate

With only about 1,100 left, Hawaiian monk seals are an endangered species and in 2012, a seal called KE18 was doing some of the endangering. It was observed attacking smaller monk seals; killing two and injuring at least 11 others. So scientists stepped in and KE18 was taken 2,000 kilometres away from his colony and housed in an aquarium . . . on his own!

Animal Assassins

Watch out for this sinister selection of animal assassins as they have murderous fun at the fairground. Quake in fear over these killer creatures who use deadly weapons to stun, kill and destroy other living things.

THE SHOCK FROM AN ELECTRIC EEL CAN KNOCK OVER A HORSE OR KILL A CAIMAN.

Owwww! That's shocking!

Dive In, If You Dare!

Electric eels are found in South American ponds and rivers. Their bodies contain around 6,000 special cells, called electrocytes, which store power like mini batteries. When they attack, all the cells discharge their electricity at the same time. This generates a burst of up to 650 volts of electricity – enough to stun or kill the fish that the eels like to feed on.

Shooting Gallery

The archerfish likes to chow down on land insects but it lives in water, so its ingenious solution is to use water as bullets. The fish fires little pellets of water out of the roof of its mouth with great force. These can knock insects up to 5 metres away off their perches and into the water.

Left a bit, right a bit ... FIRE!

TEST YOUR STING

DEADLY

INJURES SERIOUSLY

HARMFUL

OUCH

Poisonous Punch

Boxer crabs are small – many are between 2 to 3 centimetres wide – but they can certainly punch above their weight. They grip poisonous sea anemones in each claw to sting sea creatures in attack or defence.

THE ANEMONES LOOK LIKE POMPOMS BUT THEY ARE COVERED IN DEADLY STINGERS.

THE CLAW'S SNAP CREATES A SOUND AS LOUD AS A GUNSHOT. BANG!

The Grabber

Pistol shrimp have giant claws that they use to attack. The claws are almost the size of their entire 3 to 5 centimetre-long bodies! The shrimp snaps the claw shut with great force. This creates powerful blasts of pressure that can travel at speeds of up to 100 kilometres per hour to stun, or even kill, a small fish.

SNAP!

Burglars and Squatters

Pity the creatures who are victims of crime in their own homes. Other animals, sometimes of the same species, break and enter. Their aim may be to steal, or simply to squat and take over another creature's home.

Pebble Pinching Penguins

Terrible thievery sometimes happens on the Antarctic ice. Chinstrap penguins build nests out of stones they have gathered together, to protect their eggs from being carried away by water when the ice melts. However, some penguins pinch. They nip over to their neighbours' nests to steal stones for their own nests. The cheek!

Hey chick, my name's Rocky.

MALES WHO MAKE BIGGER NESTS HAVE A GREATER CHANCE OF ATTRACTING A MATE.

WATCH OUT FOR THIEVES

13 . . . 14 . . . hang on, I thought I had 15 stones in my nest.

You've got one fewer now!

Tunnel Trauma

Some shearwater birds live in New Zealand but migrate to warmer climates in the winter. When shearwaters return to their homes, they can discover a tuatara squatting in the cliff tunnels they call home. Shearwaters ignore the reptile and lay their eggs at the other end of the tunnel. All is fine until the eggs hatch . . . as baby birds are part of the tuatara's diet!

BEWARE OF SQUATTERS

It's mine now!

Oi, that's my home!

A TYPICAL MALE TUATARA IS 60 CENTIMETRES LONG AND CAN WEIGH BETWEEN ONE AND TWO KILOGRAMS.

Burrow Borrow

The burrowing owl steals the burrows of prairie dogs, armadillos or tortoises, as it can rarely be bothered to dig its own. The owl takes over the burrow and then fiercely defends its new home from the original owner.

ARMADILLO

Unwanted Guest

A cuckoo will visit another bird's nest, push out one of the eggs and lay one of its own. Once hatched, the baby cuckoo will push out other eggs or baby birds from the nest. This bad behaviour guarantees them grub at feeding time.

BURROWING OWL

Looting Lemurs

Ring-tailed lemurs on the island of Madagascar consider cicada insects to be five star foods, but they struggle to catch the crunchy critters. So, the lemurs wait until a giant wasp catches and stings a cicada, and then drags it to their underground lair. A lemur then loots the wasp's lair, stealing its meal. The rotters!

Hunger Games

Some critters turn to crime as soon as their tummies start rumbling. Hunger drives them to commit crimes ranging from shoplifting to assault, in order to satisfy their appetites.

Just dropping in for a light lunch – ha, ha!

He's going to grab my grub!

Hide-and-seek Snack

Lemurs aren't the only looters. Many creatures store their food in a place called a cache, where it is safe. Or so they think, as other creatures may be snooping around looking to steal their meals. Coyotes, for instance, love nothing more than stealing an otter's cache of caught fish.

GIANT WASPS ARE ALMOST THE SIZE OF SMALL BIRDS.

Lunch Special

CICADAS VARY IN SIZE FROM 2CM TO 5CM LONG.

Supermarket Sweep

Seagulls are infamous thieves but they usually steal from other birds. Seagull Sam, however, was one choosy criminal. In 2007, he repeatedly wandered into the same shop in Aberdeen, Scotland, and stole bags of crisps that were always the same brand and flavour (cheesy – in case you were wondering). Sam would rip open the bag outside the shop and chomp the crisps.

SOME CREATURES STEAL FOOD MOMENTS AFTER OTHERS HAVE DONE ALL THE HARD WORK COLLECTING IT. THIS SNEAKY THIEVERY IS CALLED KLEPTOPARASITISM. SEABIRDS SUCH AS SKUAS AND FRIGATEBIRDS ARE DAB HANDS AT FILCHING FISH CAUGHT BY OTHER SEABIRDS, OFTEN IN MID-AIR.

SAM BECAME SO FAMOUS THAT LOCAL PEOPLE STARTED PAYING FOR HIS ILL-GOTTEN GAINS!

Oi! Bring my bone back!

Husky Heist

Shoplifter Akira, a Siberian husky dog, thought nothing of trotting more than nine kilometres away from her home in Utah, USA, to pilfer bones from shops.

AKIRA WAS CAUGHT STEALING ON CAMERA AND BECAME AN INTERNET SENSATION.

Stop! Thief!

Not all creature thievery is about food. Some animals just cannot help themselves. They see something, want it and then take it, not caring a jot who the real owner is. Check out pickpocketing primates, a robbing roo and a light-fingered feline.

Fashion Victims

A kangaroo in Prague, Czech Republic, managed to escape from his owner and drive neighbours hopping mad by stealing underwear from their washing lines. The two-year-old roo, named Benji, was finally caught red-handed with frilly knickers!

Dusty's swag bag has included:

- 213 towels
- 73 socks
- 40 balls
- 18 shoes
- 8 bathing suits
- 2 frisbees
- 1 stuffed dinosaur

Cat Burglar

Some pet cats get used to stalking and grabbing household items instead of real-life prey. Californian cat, Dusty, is the reigning king of kitty kleptomania (repeated stealing). He's stolen more than 600 items so far!

ORANG-UTAN, CARLOS, WHO LIVES IN A ZOO IN THE PHILIPPINES, STOLE A T-SHIRT FROM A ZOO VISITOR AND THEN PUT IT ON!

What do you think, Princess?

Pilfering Primates

Orang-utans are amongst the smartest of primates but some have turned to thievery . . .

Hmmmm. It's very you, darling.

PRINCESS, AN ORANG-UTAN IN A BORNEO NATURE RESERVE, REPEATEDLY STOLE WOODEN CANOES TO PADDLE AROUND IN.

Thief In Focus

When photographer David Slater put his camera down for a few moments in a forest on the Indonesian island of Sulawesi, he hadn't taken account of some serious monkey business taking place. A crested black macaque monkey snatched the snapper and took lots of photos, including ones of himself, before Mr Slater recovered his camera.

THIS IS ONE OF THE PHOTOS THAT THE MONKEY TOOK OF HIMSELF!

I've snapped the best selfie in Sulawesi!

Con Artists

Some creatures are real confidence tricksters. They pull hustles, heists and tricks on other living things to gain food or defend themselves. Meet some of nature's best con artists.

Octopus Trick 1: Scary Stuff

The blanket octopus can pull not one, but two fast ones to defend itself. When an attacker approaches, the octopus can spread out the webbing between its arms like a giant cape, making itself look much, much bigger in size. This scares many potential predators away.

Octopus Trick 2: The Sting

If its first attempt doesn't put off the predator, the octopus tries a classic sting. Portuguese man o' war tentacles contain venom that the octopus cannot feel but that can stun and kill many other ocean dwellers. So the octopus rips off tentacles from a man o' war and then wields them as a wicked whip to protect itself.

MAN O' WAR TENTACLE ARE COVERED WITH MICROSCOPIC STINGERS CALLED NEMATOCYSTS

Lured In

Broken-rays mussels trick bass into bringing up their babies. The mussel larvae (young) attach to the bass in order to grow and travel away from their parent, so the adult mussel has a clever con. Part of it looks like a minnow fish. When a bass swims up close, hopeful of a minnow meal, the mussel sprays a cloud of larvae into the bass' face.

THE MUSSEL WIGGLES ITS FISHY LURE TO MAKE IT LOOK EVEN MORE LIKE A MINNOW FISH.

Urgh! What's this cloud getting in the way of my fish dinner?

Ouch!

Whoah!

Bandits

Now showing in the natural world near you . . .
how some varmints work in wild groups to either
defend themselves or heap misery on others.
Check out these lawless and lethal criminal networks,
which sometimes triumph over justice and fairness.

EXIT

Sorry mate, you can't leave here.

B

No Escape

Groups of tropical goatfish often take
turns in a deadly game of chase the prey.
One goatfish in a group will swim after
a smaller fish it wants to eat, such
as a seahorse, whilst others act as
blockers – sealing off escape routes
for the hapless victim. The goatfish
will swap roles so that everyone
gets a go at chasing and eating.

← GOATFISH

I've been blocked!

Major Massacre

Creatures that lack big brains and sneaky skills
use brute force and sheer numbers instead.
One species of army ant, *Eciton burchellii*,
is small (between 3 and 12 millimetres long)
but goes hunting in groups of up to 200,000
ants. The swarm of ants overwhelms and
kills almost anything in its path, including
snakes, lizards and fearsome tarantulas.

ARMY ANTS ARE ALMOST COMPLETELY
BLIND AND RELY ON VIBRATIONS, THEIR
SENSE OF TOUCH, AND CHEMICAL SCENTS
LEFT BY THE OTHERS IN THE ARMY
TO TRACK DOWN PREY.

ANT BIRDS SNEAKILY
FOLLOW THE ARMY ANTS
AND GRAB A FREE MEAL OF
ANY CREATURES KILLED OR
FLEEING THE ARMY.

AMBUSH!
Starring the coatimundi

Ambush!

Found in the Americas, the coatimundi – or coati – is a relative of the raccoon. They hunt smart, especially when tackling green iguanas, which at 1.5 metres long are up to three times their size. Some of the coatimundi climb a tree to scare a green iguana and make it leap to the forest floor, where the rest of the gang of coati are waiting to overwhelm the poor lizard.

Cripes, a coatimundi!

ANTELOPE

No Laughing Matter

Hyenas may make sounds like laughter, but quake in fear . . . for they are the ultimate bandits. Hyenas often work in groups, known as clans. Some clans send one or two hyenas into a herd of grazing animals, such as antelopes or wildebeest, to cause chaos and confusion. As the herd separates, the other hyenas target an older, younger or less speedy creature and harass it to death.

A HYENA'S HEART IS TWICE THE SIZE OF A LION'S, COMPARED TO ITS BODY WEIGHT. THIS HELPS GIVE IT THE STAMINA TO HUNT, CHASE AND HARASS PREY OVER LONG DISTANCES.

23

THE NILE PERCH CAN GROW UP TO TWO METRES LONG AND WEIGH 200 KILOGRAMS.

Big Fish

Some creatures are introduced into a new country or region and waste no time in becoming the boss. The Nile perch is one such invasive species. It was introduced into Africa's Lake Victoria in the 1950s but the giant fish soon began gobbling up almost everything else in the lake. This wiped out many other species of fish, including cichlids.

Help!

Toad Takeover

About 100 cane toads were first brought from Hawaii to Australia in 1935. They were supposed to feast on cane beetles – a major pest to Australia's sugar crop – but the toads found plenty of other things to eat. Cane toads bred rapidly and now there are more than 200 million in Australia.

Gangsters

Meet nature's mobsters and hoodlums, all trying to muscle in on the action and take over the neighbourhood. Watch out, though, as they won't let anything get in their way.

Meet The Snakehead Family

These nasty looking fish are northern snakeheads and they mean business. With their sharp teeth, they will eat almost anything that gets in their way.

FEMALE SNAKEHEADS CAN LAY UP TO 75,000 EGGS A YEAR, MEANING THAT THE SPECIES MULTIPLIES REALLY QUICKLY. THEY HAVE SPREAD FROM EAST ASIA TO WATERS IN NORTH AMERICA.

SNAKEHEADS CAN LIVE OUT OF WATER FOR UP TO FOUR DAYS AND PULL THEMSELVES OVER LAND TO FIND NEW STRETCHES OF WATER.

HE BIGGEST EVER
JE TOAD MEASURED
ENTIMETRES LONG
'D WEIGHED OVER
.6 KILOGRAMS.
BIG TROUBLE!

Hop it, punk!

CANE TOADS ARE TOXIC, SO PREDATORS THAT EAT THEM WILL DIE. AS A RESULT, THEY HAVE REDUCED POPULATIONS OF OTHER AUSTRALIAN CREATURES, SUCH AS THIS QUOLL.

25

Hooligans

From sheep getting in the way of the 2010 Tour De France cycle race to German goalie Oliver Kahn being stung by a wasp, many sporting events have been disrupted by animal hooligans. Here's a menagerie of creatures that have pitched up and made unwelcome field trips.

FOWL PLAY!

Football Fiends

Many football matches have been disrupted by animals racing across the pitch including chickens at Blackburn, squirrels at QPR and Arsenal, and a cat at the 2009 UEFA Cup Final in Turkey.

On Track

During the 2013 Bathurst 1000 race in Australia, a kangaroo leapt over the 1.8 metre-high fence and onto the track. The mad marsupial then collided with a racing car speeding at over 170 kilometres per hour. Amazingly, the kangaroo and driver were okay, but the car was too damaged to continue.

IN A 2013 SUPER LEAGUE FOOTBALL MATCH IN SWITZERLAND, A PINE MARTEN INVADED THE PITCH AND BIT ZURICH DEFENDER LORIS BENITO'S FINGERS.

Wee Are The Champions

During a 1962 World Cup match between Brazil and England, England striker, Jimmy Greaves captured a stray dog on the pitch. The dog peed over Greaves and this amused Garrincha, a Brazilian player, so much that he adopted the stray afterwards!

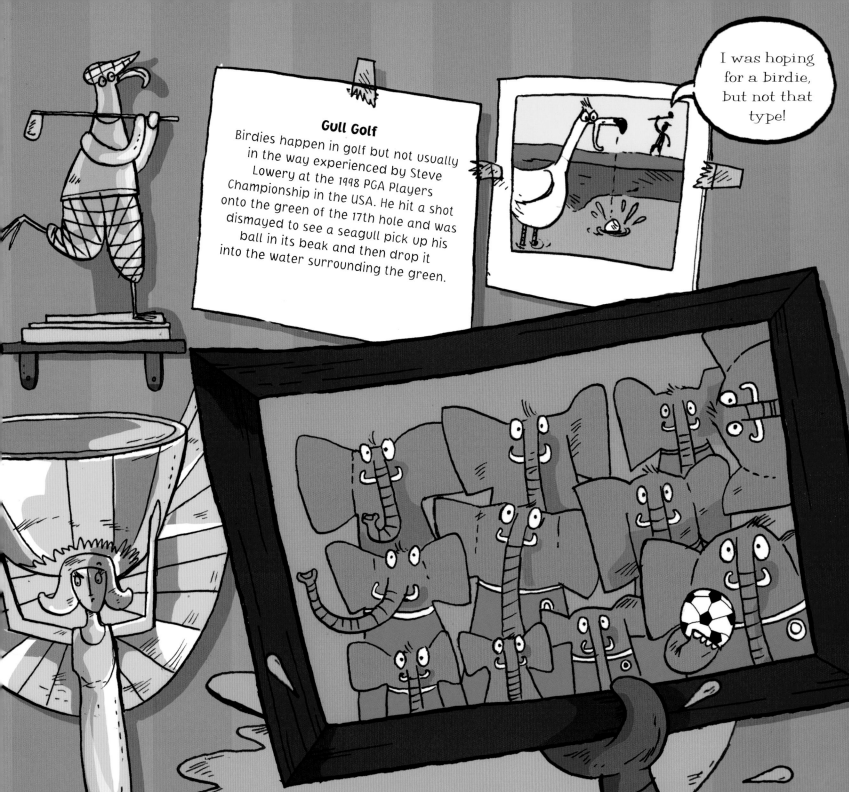

Gull Golf

Birdies happen in golf but not usually in the way experienced by Steve Lowery at the 1998 PGA Players Championship in the USA. He hit a shot onto the green of the 17th hole and was dismayed to see a seagull pick up his ball in its beak and then drop it into the water surrounding the green.

I was hoping for a birdie, but not that type!

Elephant Eleven

A herd of 11 wild elephants invaded Bisra Stadium, India, in 2013. Fortunately, the stadium was empty at the time and quick-thinking guards closed the doors. Mangos, bananas and other food were hurled over the walls until the elephants could be herded back into the jungle.

Monkey Business

Everyone loves a mischievous monkey but some characters take it too far and cause real trouble. Meet the creatures that can make a monkey out of humans.

Light-fingered Langur

At the 2010 Commonwealth Games in Delhi, India, a group of langur monkeys were trained to shoo off dogs, snakes and other wild monkeys from the sports stadiums and the athletes' rooms.

NOT ALL LANGUR MONKEYS IN INDIA ARE SO WELL BEHAVED. A GROUP OF THEM IN PUNE TURNED INTO CRIMINALS, STEALING MORE THAN 100 MOBILE PHONES FROM PEOPLE.

SOME BABOONS AREN'T CONTENT WITH JUST STEALING FOOD, THEY ALSO NICK CLOTHES, CURTAINS AND EVEN TEDDY BEARS!

Shoplifters and Burglars

The outskirts of Cape Town, South Africa, are prowled by more than 400 thieving chacma baboons. They steal food from people and shops, and some groups even clamber up apartment blocks – breaking through windows on the hunt for something to eat.

Shady Dealings

A troupe of Bolivian squirrel monkeys living at London Zoo started stealing sunglasses – right off the top of visitors' heads! Zookeepers ended up coating some other sunglasses in a bitter-tasting substance to help prevent the monkeys stealing yet more pairs.

Yuck!

IN SAFARI PARKS IN BRITAIN, RHESUS MACAQUE MONKEYS HAVE BEEN KNOWN TO HOP ONTO MOVING CARS AND GRAB BOTH A FREE RIDE AND A MOTORING SOUVENIR – RIPPING OFF CAR AERIALS, HUBCAPS OR WINDSCREEN WIPERS FOR FUN.

HAVE YOU SEEN THIS THIEVING RHESUS MACAQUE MONKEY?

Car Crime

Some baboons in Africa have become expert carjackers – they can open doors, leap through windows and even break open roof luggage holders to ransack them for food.

Vandals

Many creatures' bad behaviour is about gaining territory or finding a mate to reproduce with. Sometimes, though, creatures can't resist causing damage and mayhem to gather food or just for their own amusement. Meet some vandals who have wreaked havoc in homes, banks and aquariums.

OTTO WAS ONCE SEEN JUGGLING THE HERMIT CRABS THAT LIVED IN THE SAME TANK AS HIM.

Bad Otto

In 2008, naughty Otto the octopus learnt how to squirt water at the ceiling light over his tank in Coburg, Germany. The water caused the light to short circuit, switching off all the power in the aquarium. Otto the vandal also damaged the glass by throwing stones and rocks at it.

You Chewed

Willie the raccoon was abandoned in the wild as a baby. He was rescued and brought up by American Juan Carlos Grover. The only trouble was that Juan's home was made of wood and even when locked out, Willie thought nothing of chewing through walls to get back in. Raccoons have powerful jaws and Willie used his on cupboards, furniture and even an expensive electric guitar!

I've even got my own YouTube channel!

IN 2013, WATER LEAKS CREATED BY RODENTS MUNCHING THROUGH WATER PIPES CAUSED THE CEILING OF NAOMI RIVERA'S HOME IN FLORIDA, USA, TO CAVE IN, CAUSING OVER £20,000 OF DAMAGE.

Oops!

I hate flying... I get airsick!

Munching Money

In 2011, the State Bank of India's branch in the town of Arthur was left poorer after termites munched their way through 10 million rupees (around £100,000) of banknotes locked in the bank's safe.

I love an expensive meal!

TERMITES HAVE TINY APPETITES BUT TERMITE COLONIES CAN CONTAIN 50,000 OR MORE, SO IT DOESN'T TAKE THEM LONG TO MUNCH THROUGH ANYTHING THAT IS RICH IN CELLULOSE – SUCH AS WOOD, PLANT MATTER, CARPETS AND WALLPAPER.

Lethal Line-up

Watch out! These terrifying creatures are really hungry and are looking to add some humans to their menu. Although most creatures that attack people do so out of fear or self-defence, a fearsome few go on the attack for human snacks.

The Main Course

Whilst building a train line between Kenya and Uganda in 1898, dozens of workers were attacked and savaged by a pair of male lions. The pair avoided hunters' guns as well as lion traps for nine murderous months, until they were both shot and killed.

OVER **35** VICTIMS

OVER **30** VICTIMS

Grim and Bear It

Indian sloth bears may not be as big as grizzly bears but they make up for it with extra aggression. One sloth bear in the Mysore region of India took things too far in the 1950s, attacking more than 35 people. Twelve were killed and some other victims had their noses bitten off!

THE PAIR, NICKNAMED THE GHOST AND THE DARKNESS, WOULD CREEP INTO WORKERS' CAMPS AT NIGHT AND DRAG MEN OUT OF THEIR TENTS.

WANTED

MOST NILE CROCODILES ARE ABOUT FOUR METRES LONG BUT THE LARGEST, CALLED GUSTAVE, IS OVER SIX METRES LONG AND WEIGHS ALMOST 1,000 KILOGRAMS – AS MUCH AS A SMALL CAR.

3M

HIS ENORMOUS JAWS ARE FILLED WITH OVER 60 SHARP TEETH.

GUSTAVE'S KNOBBLY HEAD AND BODY IS MARKED WITH SCARS FROM WHERE HE HAS SURVIVED SPEARS AND FOUR GUNSHOTS.

2M

OVER 300 VICTIMS AND COUNTING!

400 VICTIMS

1M

GUSTAVE USED HIS HEFTY TAIL TO WHIP SCHOOLCHILDREN INTO THE WATER BEFORE SNACKING ON THEM.

Stripy Serial Killer

The Champawat Tiger was feared across India and Nepal in the 1890s. This 'tiger' was actually a lady – a Bengal tigress! Her killing spree began in Nepal, where she killed about 200 people. She then headed to India and killed 200 more but was stopped in her tracks by Jim Corbett, who shot her in 1907.

Shock Croc

Gustave is believed to be over 60 years old. He is said to lurk in Lake Tanganyika and the Ruzizi river, in central Africa, and is thought to have killed more than 300 people in his lifetime! Gustave was last sighted in 2008 – so has he retired or is he still out there, waiting to attack?

Creatures on Trial

All rise. The Creature Court is in session. Some living things may be naughty or dangerous, but imagine bringing an animal to a human law court to stand trial. That's precisely what happened to some unfortunate creatures in the past, even though they couldn't give evidence or understand the charges against them.

CASE FILE

CREATURE COURT

Creepy-crawly Cases

Tiny weevils eating grape vines in the French village of St Julien were put on trial in 1587. The weevils even had their own human lawyer, Pierre Rembaud. He argued in court that the insects had every right to eat. He won and the weevils not only got off, they were even given their own piece of land!

You're not roasting this rooster!

Cockerel In The Dock

A cockerel was put on trial in Switzerland in 1474 for allegedly laying an egg. The local people feared that the egg would hatch into a devilish creature and the poor cockerel was sentenced to be burnt at the stake.

Bad Bear-haviour

Even today, creatures' crimes are occasionally heard in court. In 2008, a beekeeper went to court in the Macedonian town of Bitola because a wild bear kept on raiding his beehives and stealing his honey. The court ordered the government of Macedonia to pay the beekeeper around £1,750 in damages.

THE BEAR AVOIDED CAPTURE AND COURT, BY HIDING IN THE LOCAL COUNTRYSIDE.

Grievous Bodily Ham

A sow from the French village of Savigny was taken to court in 1457 and sentenced to death for attacking a five-year-old boy. Her six piglets were also put on trial as accomplices to the crime, but were let off because they were too young.

Flee and save your bacon!

Silence in pork, I mean, court!

Run, rooster, run!

Jailbird

Lorenzo the parrot was trained to act as a lookout for drug smugglers in the Colombian city of Barranquilla. The parrot would squawk, 'Run, run, you're going to get caught!' in Spanish, alerting the criminals whenever police officers got near to their hideout. However, Lorenzo was arrested by police in 2010. He didn't have to go to court but was caged, before being handed over to animal welfare authorities.

Breakout!

Some animals in captivity might dream of escaping but only a handful get a taste of freedom. A few, such as Satara (see above) the two-tonne rhino in an Australian zoo in 2008, use brute force to smash down barriers. However, with zoo security usually tight, it often takes plenty of animal cunning to break out and get free.

Serial Offender

Los Angeles Zoo, USA, saw a staggering 35 animal breakouts in the late 1990s and early 2000s. A female gorilla called Evelyn made five of these escapes. This hairy Houdini used different escape techniques, once climbing and swinging on some vines to break free, and another time standing on the back of another gorilla, called Jim, to leap out of her enclosure.

Thanks, Jim!

JIM HIMSELF CAUGHT THE ESCAPING BUG, ONCE PULLING A DOOR OFF ITS HINGES AND SQUEEZING THROUGH A NARROW GAP TO GET FREE.

ZZZZZ

SEC

Sliding Out

In 2004, an Andean spectacled bear at Berlin Zoo, Germany, made a cheeky bid for freedom. Juan used a log as a raft to sail across the wide moat full of water that surrounded his enclosure. After climbing over a wall, on-the-run Juan didn't leave the zoo; he headed straight for its children's playground.

"JUAN WHIZZED DOWN THE SLIDE."

Walk The Plank

Sometimes, human error gives an easy escape chance, but animals still have to spot it and take it. In 1935, a worker at Frank Buck's Jungle Camp Animal Park in New York, USA, left a wooden plank across a water-filled moat at the Monkey Mountain enclosure. Capone, a rhesus monkey, soon started a great escape.

DURING THE MONKEY MAYHEM, CAPONE AND HIS CREW EVEN STOPPED A TRAIN BEFORE THEY WERE ALL RECAPTURED.

CAPONE LED MORE THAN 170 MONKEYS ACROSS THE PLANK AND OUT OF THE ZOO.

ITY

Six Days of Freedom

In 2011, an Egyptian cobra snake, called Mia, slithered out of her enclosure at Bronx Zoo in New York, USA. It took zookeepers six days to find her – she was hiding behind pipes in the reptile house.

Mmmm. *Rat*-atouille!

ZOOKEEPERS LURED MIA OUT OF HER HIDING PLACE USING WOOD SHAVINGS THAT HAD BEEN USED BY RATS AND MICE – HER FAVOURITE MEALS!

Cool Pool

Three buffalo escaped from a farm in Georgia, USA, in 2010. Two were caught quickly but the third avoided capture for over a fortnight. He was eventually found having a swim in a nearby swimming pool!

On the Run

Most escaped animals, like Rusty the red panda who bust out of the Smithsonian National Zoo in Washington, D.C. in 2013, are caught within hours. A handful of slippery critters, though, manage to stay on the run for days, weeks or months, even when there's a series of search parties out on the hunt for them.

Reggie, Steady Go!

An alligator, called Reggie, was dumped in Machado Lake, Los Angeles, USA, in 2005 when his owners couldn't handle him anymore. Despite the city spending almost 200,000 US dollars (about £130,000) tracking down Reggie, he eluded capture for 21 months!

REGGIE WAS GIVEN A NEW HOME AT LOS ANGELES ZOO, WHERE HE ALSO GAINED A GIRLFRIEND CALLED CAJUN KATE. AHHHH!

River Dance

In 1958, Cyril, a sea lion, broke out of a zoo in Canada and went on an 11-day frolic. Cyril slipped into the Thames river and made his way to Lake St Clair. He then swam down the Detroit river and into Lake Erie, crossing the Canada-USA border. Cyril was eventually found chilling out near a boathouse in Ohio, having made a 640-kilometre journey.

Crime-fighting Creatures

After reading this book, you could be forgiven for thinking that the natural world is chock full of creature criminals. Sure, there are some naughty, cheeky and downright deadly living things that harm and harass, but some creatures actually work alongside people to help fight or solve crimes.

Officer Lemon

Officer Lemon is Japan's first police cat. She can be found at Yoro police station in Kyoto, but is sometimes taken out on patrol.

LEMON IS GOOD AT COMFORTING PEOPLE WHO ARE UPSET AFTER THEY HAVE SUFFERED A BURGLARY OR HAVE RECEIVED THREATENING PHONE CALLS.

Geese Guards

In China, geese are used by farmers to protect flocks of chickens, and some geese even guard local police stations at night. These territorial birds have both keen eyesight and hearing, ideal for detecting intruders. And their loud honk is perfect for sounding the alarm.

Sniffer Rats

Since 2013, the Dutch police force have been training rats to detect suspicious smells, such as gunpowder from guns and fired bullets, and illegal drugs. The rats are cheaper to buy and quicker to teach than sniffer dogs, taking only eight to 15 days to train.

DUTCH RATS ARE GIVEN FICTIONAL POLICE NAMES, SUCH AS MAGNUM AND POIROT.

Ostrich and Emu Guards

Ostriches in Africa and emus in Australia are used to guard flocks of sheep from rustlers and wild animals that are intent on having lamb for dinner.

OSTRICH

SANTISUK HAS HIS VERY OWN UNIFORM WITH 'MONKEY POLICE' WRITTEN ON THE JACKET.

OFFICER
SANTISUK

SNIFFER RATS WORKING IN AFRICA HAVE BEEN USED TO DETECT THE CHEMICALS IN LANDMINES. THE RATS ARE LIGHT ENOUGH TO WALK OVER THE MINES WITHOUT SETTING THEM OFF. WHEN THEY DISCOVER A LANDMINE, THEY ARE GIVEN A PIECE OF BANANA.

Santisuk

A pig-tailed macaque monkey, called Santisuk, helps the police get on well with the local community. He sometimes hangs out at a police checkpoint in southern Thailand. Motorists, stuck in the checkpoint queue, cheer up when they see, play and have their photo taken with Santisuk.

Quiz and Further Reading

Are you certain you've checked out all the criminal creatures and dastardly deeds in this book? Well, put your knowledge on trial with this 20-question interrogation and see how you do. If you get 12 or more right, then you've done really, really well. But don't look back through the book or peek at the answers below; that would be criminal!

1. Is the giant Nile crocodile that has killed over 300 people called Wilfred, Gustave or Sidney?

2. Is Officer Lemon a monkey, a cat or an ostrich?

3. Is it ground squirrels, slow lorises or bottlenose dolphins that ram other creatures as they bully them?

4. Cyril the sea lion managed to escape from Canada to which country?

5. Is a hyena's heart half the size, the same size or twice the size of a lion's heart?

6. Which one of the following was not a creature that escaped from a zoo enclosure: Evelyn the gorilla, Dusty the cat or Mia the Egyptian cobra?

7. Did a kangaroo, elephant or pine marten jump onto the Bathurst 1000 motor racetrack?

8. Was Karta, Juan or Evelyn a bear that paddled on a log to escape an enclosure at Berlin Zoo?

9. What creature do boxer crabs sometimes wave around like pompoms to sting other creatures?

10. In which European city was a pet kangaroo found stealing underwear from washing lines?

11. What sort of sea creature wields stinging tentacles ripped from other creatures as a weapon?

12. Where in the slow loris' body is its venom stored?

13. What sort of creature was taken to a French court in 1587, but won their case and were given their own plot of land?

14. In which country did Sam the Seagull amuse people by pinching packets of crisps?

15. What objects do chinstrap penguins steal from each other to build their nests?

Extra Hard Questions:

16. Can you name the species of monkey that grabbed a photographer's camera and took a selfie on the Indonesian island of Sulawesi?

17. What sort of creature chewed through 10 million rupees of banknotes in a bank in India in 2011?

18. What type of fish copies the mimic octopus, looking like one of its tentacles so it can hide close to the octopus?

19. What household item has Dusty the cat stolen more of than any other thing?

20. For how many months did Reggie the alligator avoid capture for in Los Angeles?

HOW DID YOU SCORE?

16-20 WOW!

11-15 FANTASTIC!

6-10 GOOD TRY!

0-5 OUCH!

Brilliant Books

Here are some other good books to help you find out more about the lengths creatures go to in order to survive.

- *Dead or Alive?*
  Clive Gifford, Red Shed, 2014
  The ultimate guide to how creatures survive.

- *Explore the Deadly World of Bugs, Snakes, Spiders, Crocodiles*
  Barbara Taylor, Jen Green, John Farndon, Mark O'Shea, Armadillo Books, 2013
  A massive book full of information on the world's insects and reptiles, from tiny ants to massive alligators.

- *Predators*
  Steve Backshall, Orion, 2013
  A guide to the threats many creatures face to their survival.

Wonderful Weblinks

Want to find more criminal creatures? Then head to the internet and check out these weblinks.

- Uncover more kleptoparasitic creatures:
  www.bbc.co.uk/nature/adaptations/Kleptoparasitism

- Check out this sneaky spider:
  www.bbc.co.uk/nature/collections/p006r1w3#p0074tjy

- Discover an incredible fish that is brilliant at blending into the background:
  www.bbc.co.uk/nature/collections/p006r1w3#p0074tj4

Glossary

Aquarium
A single tank used for keeping fish and other creatures, or a visitor attraction containing many tanks of fish and other creatures that live in water.

Burrow
A hole or tunnel dug by an animal usually to make a home or sometimes used as a food store.

Caimans
Large water-living reptiles, related to crocodiles and alligators, which are found living in swamps and rivers in Central and South America.

Cellulose
The substance that makes up much of the walls of cells in plants.

Crop
A plant that is grown deliberately by farmers to produce either food or a useful product, such as fibres to make clothing.

Detect
To find or spot something.

Enclosure
A home for creatures in a zoo or wildlife park that is surrounded by barriers, such as walls or fences, to keep the creatures inside.

Endangered species
Creatures that are threatened with the possibility of extinction (their whole species dying out).

Feline
Creatures that belong to the cat family.

Fictional
Something that is not real but is, instead, imaginary or made up.

Great Barrier Reef
A giant coral reef, over 2,000 kilometres long in the Pacific Ocean, off the coast of Australia.

Hatch
When a bird or other creature emerges from its egg.

Illegal
Against the laws of a country.

Insects
Small creatures with six legs and with bodies formed of three parts: the head, middle section (called a thorax) and the abdomen.

Invasive species
A species of living thing that does not grow naturally in an area or region but has been introduced to the region, where it has a harmful impact on other living things.

Kleptoparasitism
A way some creatures feed by stealing food caught or gathered by other creatures.

Larvae
Newly hatched babies or junior form of creatures. Frog larvae, for instance, are tadpoles. Larvae change greatly during a stage called metamorphosis to become adults of their species.

Marsupials
Types of mammal, such as kangaroos and koalas, which give birth to underdeveloped young that continue to develop in a pouch on their mother's body.

Microscopic
Something that is so small that it can be seen clearly only when viewed under a microscope.

Migrate
To move from one area to another at different times of the year.

Moat
A deep ditch, sometimes filled with water, around the edge of some creatures' enclosures in zoos and wildlife parks.

Poison
A substance that can cause harm or death to living things through touching it, breathing it in or consuming it.

Population
The number of one type of creature, either in total across the world or in a particular place.

Predators
Creatures that hunt and feed on other creatures.

Prey
A creature hunted or caught for food.

Primates
Types of mammal including lemurs, monkeys, apes and humans that have flexible hands and feet, and highly developed brains.

Rodents
Types of mammal, including rats, mice, hamsters and squirrels, that gnaw wood and other things. Rodents have constantly growing incisor teeth.

Rustlers
People who steal other people's farm animals, particularly cattle.

Saliva
Liquid produced in a mouth to help soften and wet food as the first stages of digestion occur.

Sentenced
To receive a punishment after you have been found guilty of a crime in a law court.

Snout
The long, sticking-out jaw, nose or front part of an animal's face.

Species
A particular type of living thing. Individuals in a species can breed with each other to produce new members of their species.

Stamina
The ability of a living thing to work hard for long periods of time.

Stun
To shock or injure another living thing in some way so that it is unable to react for a little time.

Tentacle
A flexible, long and thin projection found on some creatures, such as octopuses and jellyfish.

Venom
A substance that causes harm or death when it is injected into the body of a living thing.

Index